DANIEL in the LIONS' DEN

illustrated by Leon Baxter
adapted by Belinda Hollyer

Macdonald

Daniel was just a little boy when the Persian army marched into Jerusalem. The streets were filled with shouting and Daniel was frightened, but his father explained what had happened. 'Our army has lost the war,' he said. 'We will all have to do what the Persian king tells us, for *he* is our king now.'

The Persian king took many people from Jerusalem back to Persia. He wanted them to work in his own land. So Daniel and his family had to move to Babylon, where the king had his palace.

Daniel soon settled down in the new city, for many of his friends and their families had also moved to Babylon. But his parents made sure that he did not forget their old life. 'We must obey the king,' said his father, 'but we must also remember our God. We still belong to Jerusalem – and perhaps, one day, our people will return to their real home.' So Daniel learned to pray to his own God, and live in the way his parents thought was right.

One day the king sent a servant to Daniel's house. The news he brought made Daniel's parents both pleased and sorry, for the king wanted Daniel to live at his palace, and train to work for him. Daniel's parents were pleased that their son was going to have a good job, but they were sad to lose him. 'Be good,' they said to Daniel. 'Behave yourself, and don't forget God. Do everything just as we would want you to.'

Daniel was quick and clever, and he did very well in his training. When he grew up the king made him a satrap. Satraps were the king's ministers, who helped him to rule the country. Daniel was a good man to trust, for he never made mistakes and he was honest and hardworking. Soon Daniel became one of the most powerful people in the land. Everyone said that one day, Daniel would be the king's chief adviser.

But Daniel never forgot his parents' words. He respected his king, but he was always faithful to his God as well. He prayed every day, and tried to keep God's laws as well as the king's.

The other satraps grew jealous of Daniel. They were not honest and wise like him, and they didn't like his success. When they saw how much the king liked Daniel, and how much he relied on Daniel's opinions and good sense, their jealousy turned into hatred.

'Daniel isn't even a proper Persian,' they muttered. 'Why should he be treated so well? The king would listen to *us*, if he weren't around.' And they decided to get rid of him.

It was very hard to find a way, for Daniel never did anything wrong! Everything he did worked well, and no-one ever complained about him. But one day the satraps thought of a plan. 'Daniel prays to his own God,' they said. 'Perhaps we can use that against him.' So they went to see the king.

'We think you should make sure your subjects obey you,' they said. 'We have written out a new law for you to sign. It forbids people to ask for help from anyone except you, for the next thirty days. If someone breaks the law they must be thrown into the lions' den!'

King Darius never guessed the new law was a plot against Daniel, and so he signed it. The satraps went away, smiling at one another.

Daniel knew about the new law, but he did not stop praying to his God. He could not believe it was wrong to pray. But when his enemies spied on him and saw what he was doing, they were delighted. They rushed to the king, pretending to be shocked at their discovery.

'Daniel is breaking your new law!' they cried. 'He prays to his God every day and asks for his help. But the law says no-one must ask for help except from you. Throw him to the lions!'

King Darius was dismayed, for he loved Daniel, and the last thing he wanted was to throw him to the lions. All that day he racked his brains, trying to think of a way out. But there was no way. He had signed the law, and he could not change it – not even for a friend. When the satraps returned at sunset, he had to agree to their demands.

'Very well then,' said Darius sadly. 'Daniel will have to go to his death. But how I wish I'd never signed that law!'

King Darius and Daniel walked together in silence through
the vast palace and across the gardens. At last they reached
the far corner of the palace grounds where the lions' den
was. Savage roars could be heard from inside the den, for
the lions were hungry. Their evening meal had not been fed
to them: Daniel was to be their dinner instead.

Daniel stood quietly in the evening light and looked at his
king. He knew it was not Darius' fault that all this had
happened. 'I have served you honestly, King Darius,' he
said softly. 'Think well of me when I am dead.'

'If I could save you from this death, I would do so,'
answered Darius. 'But since I cannot, ask your God to help
you. You have been faithful to him for years, and it is
because of that faith that you are in such danger. Pray to
him now, Daniel!'

Daniel nodded. Then he turned, and walked into the
den. The entrance was sealed with a stone, and Darius
returned to the palace in despair. He could not believe he
would ever see Daniel again.

Daniel tried to feel brave when he entered the lions' den, but it was almost impossible. His legs shook as he walked down the long passageway into the den. He was not a warrior – and even if he had been, what chance would he have had against lions, with only his bare hands to protect himself?

The den was carved from solid rock, with only a tiny barred window. It took Daniel's eyes a few moments to get used to the gloom, but when they did he could see the lions quite clearly. There were six of them, crouching like shadows against the walls. Their yellow eyes glinted as they turned to look at Daniel. They licked their lips in silence, and prowled across the den towards him.

Daniel tried to swallow, but his throat was dry with fear. He sank to his knees and closed his eyes. The lions' great paws padded softly on the rock, but he could tell that they were drawing closer. As they circled him, they growled. Daniel felt their hot breath on his face, and pictured their sharp fangs. He shuddered hopelessly. 'I have only a moment or two of life left to me,' he thought. 'What shall I do?'

Just then, Daniel remembered King Darius' words. 'Ask your God to help you,' the king had said, and Daniel suddenly felt a rush of hope. God had helped him in the past, and all his prayers had been answered up to now. If anyone could save him from the lions' jaws, it was God.

So Daniel stood up, took a deep breath, and began to pray. 'God, you are my only hope!' he cried. 'Save me from the lions tonight!' Then he raised his arms into the air, and started to sing. His voice filled the pit with music as he sang praises to God – and that very moment, the lions drew back. God had heard Daniel, and answered his prayer!

The lions stopped growling, forgot their hunger, and lay down around Daniel. Their eyes narrowed and closed with pleasure as they listened to him sing. Then a low rumbling noise joined Daniel's voice, and the lions began to purr.

Darius sat up all that night. He had never been so miserable before – for he was a rich and powerful king, who had always got what he wanted. He had a wonderful palace, beautiful wives and lovely children, and the very best of everything that Persia could offer. But now he realised that the one thing he wanted more than anything was to save his friend – and that seemed impossible.

Darius tried to sleep, but he could not. His servants brought food and wine, but he sent it all away. When the anxious palace staff peered through his doorway they saw their king tossing and turning on his bed, or leaping to his feet and pacing the floor.

'Oh Daniel,' he muttered in distress, 'ask your God to save you from the lions!'

As soon as the first dawn light broke the night sky, Darius left the palace. He stumbled across the gardens, almost despairing, yet still hoping that the impossible would have happened, and that Daniel might still be alive.

Inside the den Daniel stopped praying, and opened his eyes.
He could hear King Darius outside, calling to him. 'Daniel!'
the faint shout said. 'Daniel, has your God saved you?'

Daniel looked around him, and saw that the lions were
asleep on the floor. They stretched like giant kittens when
they heard the king's voice. Then they tucked their noses
into their paws, and went back to sleep.

Daniel reached the mouth of the den just as the stone was
pulled away. Tears came to Darius' eyes when he saw his
friend step out into the morning sunlight, and he hugged
him joyfully.

'God answered my prayers,' laughed Daniel. 'He kept me safe all night. Look, I'm not even scratched!'

Darius was so impressed with the power of Daniel's God that he sent messengers all over the world to tell people what had happened. He said everyone should worship Daniel's God, who had saved him when no human could do so. Then the king threw the wicked satraps who had plotted against Daniel into the lions' den. This time, no-one came out alive.

This story has been told in many different ways for more than two thousand years. It was first written down in a language called Aramaic. Since then it has been re-told in almost every language used in the world today.

You can find the story of Daniel in the Lions' Den in the Bible. It is in the Book of Daniel, Chapter 6.